AGATHA WHISKEY

50 Cocktails
to Celebrate the
Bestselling Novelist
of All Time

COLLEEN MULLANEY
PHOTOGRAPHY BY
JACK DEUTSCH

Skyhorse Publishing

Skyhorse Publishing books may be purchased in bulk at special discounts for sales promotion, corporate gifts, fund-raising, or educational purposes. Special editions can also be created to specifications. For details, contact the Special Sales Department, Skyhorse Publishing, 307 West 36th Street, 11th Floor, New York, NY 10018 or info@skyhorsepublishing.com.

Skyhorse® and Skyhorse Publishing® are registered trademarks of Skyhorse Publishing, Inc.®, a Delaware corporation.

Visit our website at www.skyhorsepublishing.com.

10 9 8 7 6 5 4 3 2 1

Library of Congress Cataloging-in-Publication Data is available on file.

Edited by Nicole Mele
Interior design by Chris Schultz
Cover design by Kai Texel
Cover photos by Jack Deutsch

Print ISBN: 978-1-5107-7595-4
Ebook ISBN: 978-1-5107-7596-1

Printed in China

For Trisha
To have such a creative, funny, and honest friend is a gift.
To have such a creative, funny, and honest friend who sits at the bar with you
sipping cocktails while brainstorming about cocktails is winning.

TABLE OF CONTENTS

FOREWORD

"What's your poison?"

So begins many a boozy adventure, but this also happens to be an excellent way to approach an Agatha Christie novel. The Queen of Crime used poisons more than any other means to murder her characters. Fail to pay attention to what you're imbibing in a Christie mystery, and you very well may find yourself—well, written out of the story.

Of course, alcohol itself is an excellent vehicle for poison, given its ubiquity, its tendency to be ingested quickly, and its strong flavor, which can be used to overpower a bitter taste. Take the setup at the start of *Three Act Tragedy* (1934), in which the renowned stage actor Sir Charles Cartwright serves cocktails to his guests, only for one of them—a man of the cloth, no less—to fall dead. And let's never forget the debauched crew of Bright Young Things at the center of *Peril at End House* (1932), who could get up to all sorts of mischief with a muddler, a strainer, and a cocktail pick or two. Of course, it's often "the help" who do the mixing and serving. But we would do best to heed the advice of both Monsieur Poirot and Miss Marple, Christie's two most famous detectives, and never underestimate the crucial role these servants play, all while balancing multiple drinks on a tray.

The most famous drink in the Christie canon is probably the champagne referenced in the very title of *Sparkling Cyanide* (1945). Not once, but *twice*, does a glass of bubbly turn deadly at the swanky Luxembourg night club. But I prefer the alcohol-soaked scene Christie sets in *The Mirror Crack'd from Side to Side* (1962). There's a party on at Gossington Hall, a traditional country estate we've seen in previous Miss Marple stories, but which is now the lavish (read: heavily renovated) home of Hollywood actress Marina Gregg. And the drinks, they are a-flowin':

(continued . . .)

gin martinis, some vodka concoction one character advises another should be "thrown straight down the throat," and a daiquiri that a starstruck fan accepts from Marina herself. ("I've had three already," admits the movie star.) Alas, the drink does not agree with Marina's number one fan, and the poor woman dies soon after downing it.

Five Little Pigs (1942), which I believe to be the best novel Christie ever wrote, features a character whose habit of drinking a full bottle of beer all in one go does him no favors. But in *Passenger to Frankfurt* (1970), Christie takes matters a step further, with an inciting incident in which our hero *knowingly* drinks from an open glass of beer that's been drugged by a woman he just met, for purposes of knocking him unconscious so that she can board a plane under his name and thereby evade the people she claims want to kill her. (I mean, it *was* the seventies, after all.)

Is it any wonder Monsieur Poirot tends to stick to his fruit-flavored sirops, or that Miss Marple brews her own damson gin and cherry brandy in the comfort—and safety—of her home? What is a mystery-loving tippler to do?

Thank goodness for Colleen Mullaney, who is here to lay it all out for us: fifty cocktails inspired by the mysteries of the world's bestselling author. My lips are already puckering in anticipation.

But wait! I can hear some of you say. *Wasn't Agatha Christie a teetotaler?* Indeed, she was. Alcohol didn't agree with her, so she generally abstained. This is why Colleen has provided mocktail alternatives for each of her recipes, in a loving nod to Christie's preference. I have to imagine Dame Agatha would have approved and held up her glass to cheers the book you're about to read, preferred drink in hand: a cup of cream, served neat. (Shudder.)

That was Christie's poison. What's yours?

—Kemper Donovan,
mystery author and host of the *All About Agatha* podcast

PART I

BAR BASICS

Just as having the proper tools can assist in gathering clues and solving a case, these bar basics are vital to making a world-class cocktail. Like writing a perfectly penned story, the keys to creating an exquisite cocktail are shaking the components or stirring them in dramatic fashion and then straining or editing what is not needed. Gather and use the right tools and ingredients from your cocktail cabinet and delicious drinks are a sure result.

Barspoon
These long-handled spoons, often featuring a spiral shaft, allow you to crack and shape ice and to stir a cocktail in a mixing glass elegantly.

Blender
Use a stick or immersion blender for preparing liquid ingredients and a countertop model for ice and frozen cocktails.

Jigger
As in crime solving, precision is essential. Invest in a double-sided jigger with fractions marked inside the measuring cups for easy mixing.

Juicer
Fresh juice is essential for adding zesty character to a cocktail. I love a hand press for up to four cocktails, but for larger batch cocktails, electric juicers are the way to go.

Mixing Glass
Like a good mystery, the right atmosphere is crucial for mixing different components. Look for mixing glasses that can fit the top of a shaker inside the rim for versatility.

(continued . . .)

Muddler

Just as Hercule Poirot disdains those who "muddle" in his cases, a culinary muddler releases oils, aromas, and juices of herbs, fruits, and vegetables.

Shakers

The right shaker can unlock a world of cocktails. They are even good for whipping cream to top cocktails. Styles include the Boston (a pint glass topped with a shaking tin; the cobbler (with a cap over the strainer, which fits into the bottom tin); the Parisian (two stainless steel tins that join); and the weighted shaker (in which the smaller tin on top fits into the larger tin on the bottom).

Strainers

Like separating the innocent from the suspicious characters in Agatha's novels, strainers are imperative for separating seeds, bits, pieces, and melted ice from cocktails. A Hawthorne strainer—with a flat top, central perforations, and a metal spiral around the edge—fits snugly into the large tin of any shaker and allows you to adjust the straining level by pushing the spiral forward. A julep strainer has a perforated metal bowl with a handle and will fit snuggly into a mixing glass to strain stirred drinks. A fine mesh strainer is also useful for cocktails.

Torch

Small handheld butane kitchen torches add drama and mystique to cocktail garnishes. They can be used to smoke the tips of rosemary sprigs or ends of cinnamon sticks and caramelize citrus slices, all while releasing their aromas and flavors for an elevated cocktail experience.

Y-Shaped Vegetable Peeler

This design safely allows you to make proper twists for garnishes (and plots!).

GLASSWARE

Just as the weapon must fit the crime, the glass must fit the cocktail. I'm a big fan of mix and match, but investing in a set or two of these essential glasses ensures that you're always ready for mixing in style:

 Champagne Flute

 Collins Glass

 Wine Glass

 Coupe Glass

 Martini Glass

 Julep Cup

 Rocks Glass

SYRUPS

Syrups can add a distinct layer of flavor to cocktails and mocktails. Easy to make with endless combinations of spices, herbs, fruits, and vegetables, they elevate your libations in a natural, fresh, organic way.

Basic Simple Syrup

> 1 cup water
>
> 1 cup sugar

In a saucepan, combine all ingredients and bring to a boil, stirring until the sugar dissolves. Remove the saucepan from the heat. The syrup will keep in an airtight container in the refrigerator for up to one month.

Rhubarb Syrup

> 1 cup water
>
> 1 cup sugar
>
> 2 cups chopped rhubarb
>
> 1 teaspoon vanilla extract

In a saucepan, combine the water, sugar, and rhubarb and bring to a boil. Reduce heat, simmer for 15 minutes, and remove the saucepan from the heat. Once cooled, add in the vanilla extract, pour the mixture into a blender or food processor, and blend until smooth. Strain through a fine mesh sieve into an airtight container. The syrup will keep in the refrigerator for up to one month.

Mint Simple Syrup

> 1 cup water
>
> 1 cup sugar
>
> 10–15 mint leaves

In a saucepan, combine the water and sugar and bring to a boil, stirring until the sugar dissolves. Remove the saucepan from the heat, add in the mint leaves, and let steep for 30 minutes (or up to 2 hours). Strain the syrup into an airtight container, and keep in the refrigerator for up to one month.

Honey Syrup

    1 cup water

    1 cup sugar

    ¾ cup honey

In a saucepan, combine all ingredients and bring to a boil, stirring until the sugar dissolves. Remove the saucepan from the heat. The syrup will keep in an airtight container for up to one month.

Winter Spice Syrup

    1 cup water

    1 cup sugar

    3 cinnamon sticks

    ⅛ cup allspice berries

    6 cloves

    2 star anise

In a saucepan, combine the water and sugar and bring to a boil, stirring until the sugar dissolves. Reduce heat to a simmer and add in the cinnamon sticks, allspice berries, cloves, and star anise. Simmer for 10 minutes, remove the saucepan from the heat, and let mixture steep for 30 to 60 minutes. Strain syrup into an airtight container, and keep in the refrigerator for up to one month.

(continued . . .)

Rose Simple Syrup

        1 cup water
        1 cup sugar
        2 cups rose petals from organic, pesticide-free roses
        2 hibiscus leaves to give syrup a nice deep pink color

In a saucepan, combine the water and sugar and bring to a boil, stirring until the sugar dissolves. Reduce heat to a simmer and add in the rose petals and hibiscus leaves. Simmer for 10 minutes, remove the saucepan from the heat, and let the mixture steep for 10 minutes. Strain syrup into an airtight container, and keep in the refrigerator for up to one month.

Tarragon Simple Syrup

        1 cup water
        1 cup sugar
        1 cup tarragon leaves

In a saucepan, combine the water and sugar and bring to a boil, stirring until the sugar dissolves. Add in the tarragon leaves and remove the saucepan from the heat. Let the mixture steep for 20 minutes, then strain into an airtight container. The syrup will keep in the refrigerator for up to one month.

Lemon Simple Syrup

        ½ cup water
        1 cup sugar
        Juice of 3 lemons
        Peel of 1 lemon

In a saucepan, combine the water, sugar, and lemon juice. Bring to a boil, stirring until the sugar dissolves. Remove the saucepan from the heat and add in the lemon peel. Let the mixture steep for 30 minutes, then strain into an airtight container. The syrup will keep in the refrigerator for up to one month.

Honey Rosemary Simple Syrup

1 cup water
½ cup honey
2 sprigs rosemary

In a saucepan, bring all ingredients to a boil, simmer for 5 minutes, then remove the saucepan from the heat and let the mixture steep for up to 30 minutes. Strain syrup into an airtight container, and keep in the refrigerator for up to two weeks.

Blackberry-Hibiscus Simple Syrup

1 cup sugar
1 cup water
½ cup blackberries
½ cup dried hibiscus flowers

In a saucepan, bring all ingredients to a boil and simmer for 5 minutes while muddling the blackberries. Once the sugar fully dissolves, remove the saucepan from the heat and let the mixture steep for up to 30 minutes. Strain syrup into an airtight container, and keep in the refrigerator for up to one month.

TECHNIQUES

Dry Shake

A dry shake is simply shaking your ingredients without ice. For cocktails that call for egg whites, this technique ensures a thick and frothy top to any cocktail: First, shake the egg whites without any ice. This lets the protein in the egg foam up instead of becoming diluted from the ice in the shaker. Second, add the rest of the cocktail ingredients to the shaker and shake with ice to chill the cocktail and strengthen the foam. Strain the cocktail into a glass, take the top off the shaker, and add any extra foam to the top of your cocktail with a barspoon.

Build

Add the ingredients in the order specified directly into a serving glass.

Roll

Roll or transfer a cocktail from one vessel, such as a bar glass, to another to prevent over dilution. Bloody Marys are often made using the rolling technique.

Strain

Using a fine mesh sieve or strainer, straining removes any solids, seeds, or pulp from a cocktail.

Garnish

This is a cocktail's finishing touch, where the mystery comes together. I love a garnish and use a variety of ingredients such as herbs, edible flowers, fruits, berries, and tomatoes to add color, texture, aroma, and flavor to any cocktail. Citrus twists, spirals, wedges, and wheels add oils, juices, and vibrant color. Chocolate, cinnamon, and nutmeg add aroma and give a hint of what's to come in the glass. There is really no limit here, so choose the garnish that correlates best with the ingredients in your cocktail.

Float

Pour liquid over the back of a barspoon into a serving glass to add a top layer to your cocktail.

Rim

Rim your glass with salty or sweet toppings to add extra flavor to your drink. The most common are salt and sugar, but chocolate, caramel, and peppermint bits are all fun ideas. Start by coating the rim of your glass. If salting or sugaring the rim, rub a wedge of citrus around it first, then dip the rim in a shallow plate of coarse salt or sugar. For more elaborate rims, melt chocolate (milk, dark, or white) or caramel and coat the rims liberally. Dip rims in toppings such as crushed candy. Set to dry.

PART II

DRINKING DETECTIVES

Agatha's characters are a grand collection of different personalities. To include them all would require cocktails for days and days, so we celebrate her central characters Hercule Poirot and Miss Marple, while including a few of the more colorful sidekicks.

Hercule Poirot

Pronounced "pwaro," Poirot is one of Agatha's most famous and long-lived characters, appearing in thirty-three novels and fifty-nine short stories. He is a world-renowned Belgian private detective, unsurpassed in his intelligence and understanding of the criminal mind, both respected and admired by police forces and heads of state across the globe. Equally famous for his magnificent moustache and his "little grey cells," he loves order and symmetry and despises mess and disarray. Hercule has been portrayed on screen by various actors including Albert Finney, Peter Ustinov, Ian Holm, Tony Randall, Alfred Molina, David Suchet, and Kenneth Branagh. Hercule Poirot became the only fictional character ever to be honored with an obituary on the front page of *The New York Times*.

Miss Marple

Miss Jane Marple doesn't look like your average detective. She doesn't look like a detective at all. Having spent her entire life in the small village of St. Mary Mead, she is surprisingly worldly, with an uncanny way of observing everything around her as she blends into the background. Miss Marple is an avid knitter, gardener—and gossip. Because

(continued . . .)

she is unassuming and often overlooked, she has the freedom to pursue the truth without gaining anyone's attention, especially criminals, and uses her sixth sense and abilities to observe human nature to solve the most difficult of crimes.

Adriadne Oliver

A renowned writer of crime, Oliver accompanies Hercule on several of his more famous cases (*The Pale Horse*, *The Hollow*, *Third Girl*), using her astute female intuition to help solve the crimes.

Chief Inspector Japp

In the early years, Hercule made things difficult for Japp when he would contradict Japp's conclusion on a case, but through the years they became trusted friends, helping each other on several cases (*The Mysterious Affair at Styles*, *Peril at End House*, *The ABC Murders*).

Parker Pyne

Pyne is not really a detective at all, but rather specializes in detecting and curing unhappiness. Known affectionately as the "heart specialist," Pyne appears in fourteen short stories (*Problem at Pollensa Bay and Other Stories*).

AGATHA WHISKEY

◆

Serves 2

Agatha Christie wrote her first novel, The Mysterious Affair at Styles, *at the age of twenty-six, as a bet she had with her sister Madge. Although she had written a few short stories, this was her first detective novel. Her success was far from immediate, finding rejection from four publishers before being offered a contract. During the first world war, Agatha worked as an assistant dis-penser, gaining knowledge of poisons, and a few years* later passed her apothecary exam in London with a degree from the Worshipful Society of Apothecaries. This expertise (or "poison proficiency") was put to good use; out of her sixty-six murder mysteries, poison was the cause of death for more than thirty characters.

Dame Agatha Christie
© Shutterstock

- 2 ounces bourbon whiskey
- 2 ounces blackberry juice
- 1 ounce blackberry liqueur
  - (I recommend Heimat New York Blackberry)
- 1 ounce Mint Simple Syrup (page 6)
- 1 egg white
- Blackberries and mint sprigs for garnish

In a shaker filled with ice, combine all ingredients. Shake well until chilled and frothy. Strain evenly between two glasses, take top off the shaker, and spoon froth on top of each glass. Garnish each glass with a blackberry and mint sprig and serve.

Mocktail

Replace whiskey with Kentucky 74 or another nonalcoholic spirit, add 1 ounce additional blackberry juice, and prepare as above.

HERCULE'S HURRICANE

◆

Serves 2

The Mysterious Affair at Styles *was Agatha's first published novel and introduces the infamous, eccentric Belgian detective Hercule Poirot. The novel takes place in Styles Court, a beautiful, isolated country manor outside Essex, England. The story reads like a revolving whodunit with every house guest a suspect, all with something to hide. Between the widower (is his grieving genuine?), the greedy stepchildren, the housekeeper, and the other houseguests, the accusations fly like a hurricane.*

> 4 ounces dark rum (I recommend Plantation)
> 2 ounces light rum (I recommend Plantation)
> 4 ounces blood orange juice
> 4 ounces pineapple juice
> 4 dashes blood orange bitters
>   (I recommend Stirrings Blood Orange Bitters)
> Blood orange slices and rosemary sprigs for garnish

In a shaker filled with ice, combine all ingredients. Strain into ice-filled glasses. Garnish with blood orange slices and rosemary sprigs.

Mocktail

Replace the rums with Ritual Rum Alternative Zero Proof or another nonalcoholic spirit. Prepare as above for a hurricane without the aftermath!

MISS MARPLE'S CHERRY BLOSSOM

◆

Serves 2

Miss Jane Marple's character is based loosely on Agatha's grandmother and her friends, and has appeared in twelve novels and twenty short stories. She makes her own cherry brandy from her garden, claiming that a bit of brandy helps ease one's nerves. Cheers to that, Jane!

1 ounce gin (I recommend Wölffer)
1 ounce cherry brandy
1 ounce sake
¾ ounce grenadine
1 ounce lemon juice
Edible flowers for garnish

In a shaker with ice, combine all ingredients. Shake well, strain into coupe glasses, garnish with edible flowers, and serve.

Mocktail

Replace the gin with Monday or another nonalcoholic spirit, the cherry brandy with San Pellegrino's Sanbitter Red or another nonalcoholic aperitif, and the sake with Gekkeiken alcohol-free Daiginjo Sake or another nonalcoholic sake. Prepare as above.

THEY DO IT WITH MARGARITAS

(They Do It with Mirrors)

❖

Serves 2

Ruth van Rydock, concerned about her sister Carrie Louise's well-being after she received a death threat, contacts old schoolmate Miss Marple asking for help. During a blackout on the evening of her arrival, several gunshots are heard, and a man is found dead in his room. Soon after, two people are killed by falling stage weights. These events set Miss Marple on a quest to find out what is really going on before the scene turns deadly once again. Uncover the truth with this spicy cocktail!

> 4 slices jalapeño pepper, deseeded
> 2 ounces fresh lime juice
> 4 ounces tequila
> 2 ounces Cointreau
> 2 ounces pineapple juice
> Tajín (5 tablespoons red chili powder; 1 tablespoon fresh lime
>   zest, oven-dried; 1 tablespoon sea salt) to rim glasses
> Pineapple and lime wedges for garnish

In a bar glass, muddle the jalapeño pepper and lime juice. Add in the tequila, Cointreau, and pineapple juice. Fill bar glass with ice and shake well. Pour into Tajín-rimmed glasses, garnish with pineapple and lime wedges, and serve.

Mocktail

Replace the tequila with Ritual Tequila Alternative or another nonalcoholic spirit and the Cointreau with Lyre's Italian Orange or another nonalcoholic aperitif. Prepare as above.

BLOODY MARY IN THE LIBRARY

(The Body in the Library)

---◆---

Serves 2

Good morning, there is a body in the library! It's seven in the morning and the body of a dead girl is found in the Bantrys' library. She is wearing an evening dress and heavy makeup smeared across her cheeks. Coffee, please! Who is she and how did she get there? Colonel Arthur Bantry and his wife, Dolly, invite their dear friend Miss Marple to help solve the case before the gossip mill goes nuts. The girl, they find out, was a dancer at the Majestic Seaside Hotel. Being the doers they are, Dolly and Jane decide to take a suite at the hotel to investigate further. Back at home, just as a second girl's charred remains are found in a quarry, the Bantrys' eccentric neighbor is being questioned, but did he murder the girl or just dump her body in the study as a sick joke? As the ladies take cocktails in the lounge, they observe a little more than dirty dancing and unscrupulous card playing. It's time for this dynamic duo to set a trap and catch the cold-blooded murderer. Remember to pick your partner well; no one puts baby in the corner.

> 1 pinch black pepper + extra to rim glasses
>
> 1 pinch celery salt + extra to rim glasses
>
> 6 ounces vodka
>
> 8 ounces tomato juice or V8®
>
> 2 teaspoons horseradish sauce
>
> 1 ounce fresh lemon juice
>
> 1 pinch paprika
>
> 2 dashes Worcestershire sauce (I recommend Lea & Perrins)
>
> Celery stalks, cucumber slices, and cherry tomatoes for garnish

(continued . . .)

If desired, rim two Collins glasses with a mixture of black pepper and celery salt and set aside. In a bar glass filled halfway with ice, combine all ingredients. Pour into another bar glass and pour back and forth between the two glasses 4 to 6 times (see Roll on page 10). Strain into two Collins glasses filled halfway with ice. Garnish with celery stalks, cucumber slices, and cherry tomatoes. Serve.

Mocktail

Replace the vodka with Monday or another nonalcoholic spirit and prepare as above.

MOVING BUTTERY FINGER

(The Moving Finger)

◆

Serves 2

Agatha Christie considered The Moving Finger *one of her best novels. While some stories don't stand the test of time, this one surely does. The charming village of Lymstock seems the perfect place for Jerry Burton to recuperate from his accident under the care of his sister, Joanna. But a series of scandalous rumors sent by a mystery writer soon accuses residents of despicable things, resulting in one resident's unfortunate suicide. As the tensions escalate, Miss Marple shows up to avenge one of the victims, her beloved former maid. Can she find the poison pen writer before another tragedy unfolds?*

4 ounces dark chocolate to rim glasses

2 ounces butterscotch liqueur

2 ounces Kahlúa

2 ounces vanilla vodka

1 ounce Baileys Irish cream

Crushed Butterfinger candy for garnish

Rim two stemless Martini glasses with chocolate by using a double boiler or a microwave oven on low to melt the dark chocolate. Pour onto a shallow plate and dip the rims of the glasses in the chocolate to coat. Let dry. In a shaker filled with ice, combine all ingredients and shake well. Strain into stemless Martini glasses. Serve.

Mocktail

Replace the butterscotch liqueur with Torani Butterscotch Syrup or another butterscotch syrup, the Baileys with coffee creamer, the Kahlúa with DaVinci Gourmet or another coffee-flavored syrup, and the vodka with Monday or another nonalcoholic spirit. Prepare as above.

PASSION FRUIT MARTINIS ARE ANNOUNCED

(A Murder Is Announced)

---◆---

Serves 2

Agatha's fiftieth book, A Murder Is Announced, *was highly publicized and is often considered a staple of crime fiction and the best of all Miss Marple novels. Miss Marple, on holiday in nearby Medenham Wells, is ably assisted by Inspector Craddock. The villagers of Chipping Cleghorn are bursting with curiosity over an advertisement in the local gazette that reads, "A murder is announced and will take place on Friday, October 29th, at Little Paddocks at 6:30 p.m." Unable to resist, a crowd gathers at the appointed time. Suddenly, the lights go out and a gunshot explodes. A novel of redemption, this story has more motives than a well-greased hinge, and no one is who they seem. If invited, would you go?*

3 ounces vodka

2 ounces passion fruit liqueur

6 ounces passion fruit nectar

1 ounce fresh lime juice

Fresh passion fruit slices for garnish

In a shaker filled with ice, combine the vodka, passion fruit liqueur and nectar, and lime juice. Mix until well-chilled and frothy. Strain into coupe glasses, garnish with passion fruit slices, and serve.

Mocktail

Replace the vodka with Seedlip Grove 42 or another nonalcoholic spirit and the liqueur with Belvoir Passion Fruit Martini or another nonalcoholic passion fruit liqueur. Prepare as above.

"I won't stand for wickedness. Wickedness has to be destroyed."

—Agatha Christie, *A Pocket Full of Rye*

A POCKET FULL OF ROSÉ

(A Pocket Full of Rye)

◆

Serves 2

A classic case of crime by rhyme. When Rex Fortescue and his wife are killed in quick succession, the Fortescues' maid Gladys calls in her previous employer, Miss Marple, to help her bring the killer to justice. Miss Marple soon realizes that the series of murders follow a nursery rhyme, "Sing a Song of Sixpence." Rex was found dead in his counting house with a pocketful of rye grain, his wife in the parlor eating bread and honey, and the maid in the yard hanging out the clothes, where she is found with a clothespin over her nose. Dead blackbirds found on the property and on Rex's desk serve as a reminder of his past sins at the Blackbird Mine in east Africa. Someone is out for revenge, and killing fast. Let's sort that out over a pocket full of rosé!

    2 ounces cognac
    1 ounce Rose Simple Syrup (page 8)
    1 ounce lemon juice
    4 dashes lemon bitters
        (I recommend Fee Brothers Lemon Bitters)
    Sparkling rosé to top glasses
    Fresh rose petals for garnish

In a shaker filled with ice, combine the cognac, Rose Simple Syrup, lemon juice, and bitters. Shake out the wickedness or until well-chilled. Strain into glasses and top with sparkling rosé. Garnish with fresh rose petals and serve.

Mocktail

Replace the sparkling rosé with Wölffer Estate Spring in a Bottle or another nonalcoholic wine, the cognac with Seedlip Grove 42 or another nonalcoholic spirit, and the bitters with All The Bitter New Orleans Bitters or other nonalcoholic bitters. Prepare as above.

SPARKLING CYANIDE

(Sparkling Cyanide)

---◆---

Serves 2

Champagne as a murder weapon? Tragic, indeed! A celebratory dinner turns deadly when a beautiful heiress is fatally poisoned in a Luxembourg restaurant. Her death is ruled a suicide until her grieving husband, George, receives letters suggesting otherwise. Taking matters into his own hands, George recreates that fateful dinner party—complete with a champagne toast. Six people sit down at a table set for seven, and in front of the empty place is a sprig of rosemary in solemn memory of Rosemary Barton, who died at the same table exactly one year ago. Will it be a repeat affair? Only the bubbles hold the key to this murder mystery.

2 ounces elderflower liqueur (I recommend Heimat)

2 ounces gin (I recommend Wölffer)

Honey Rosemary Simple Syrup (page 9)

Brut champagne to top glasses

Rosemary sprigs for garnish

In a small pitcher, combine the elderflower liqueur, gin, and Honey Rosemary Simple Syrup. Pour into flute glasses until ⅓ full. Top with champagne, garnish with rosemary sprigs, and serve.

Mocktail

Replace the champagne with Chateau de Fleur or another nonalcoholic sparkling wine, the elderflower liqueur with Root Elixirs Cucumber Elderflower Sparkling Mixers or another nonalcoholic elderflower beverage, and the gin with Monday or another nonalcoholic spirit.

"The happy people are failures because they are on such good terms with themselves that they don't give a damn."

—Agatha Christie, *Sparkling Cyanide*

POIROT'S WHITE CHRISTMAS

(Hercule Poirot's Christmas)

Serves 2

Holidays are anything but merry when a family reunion is marred by murder. Wealthy Simeon Lee invites his family home for Christmas and abruptly announces that he is cutting them out of his will. When the patriarch is found brutally murdered hours later, suspicion falls on every member of this dysfunctional family. Hercule Poirot, who is staying in the same snow-covered village with a friend, offers his assistance and quickly finds that everyone has a reason to hate the old man. As secrets of deception and murder in Africa long ago come to light, they shine like the missing diamonds from Simeon's safe.

- 3 ounces vanilla vodka
- 3 ounces white chocolate liqueur
- 2 ounces peppermint schnapps
- 1½ ounces heavy cream
- Whole nutmeg, grated, for garnish

In a shaker filled with ice, combine all ingredients. Shake well to work out any family issues. Strain into glasses. Garnish with grated nutmeg and serve.

Mocktail

Replace the vodka with Monday or another nonalcoholic spirit, the white chocolate liqueur with Ghirardelli White Chocolate sauce or another white chocolate sauce, the peppermint schnapps with ½ ounce peppermint extract, and increase the heavy cream to 2 ounces. Prepare as above.

MURDERS & MYSTERIES
IN FARAWAY PLACES

A gatha loved exploring different places, reveling in her surround-ings, and collecting a wealth of knowledge that she would later use in her writing. She visited South Africa, Australia, New Zealand, Canada, and North America. She traveled further with her second hus-band, Sir Max Mallowan, a prominent British archeologist specializing in ancient Middle Eastern history, to more exotic locations like Iraq, Syria, and Egypt. Her love of new places and attention to detail come across on the pages of her novels, plays, and short stories.

ROGER'S RICKEY

(The Murder of Roger Ackroyd)

---◆---

Serves 2

A wealthy widow overdoses and turns the peaceful English village of King's Abbot upside down. Her fiancé (and King Abbot's wealthiest citizen) Roger Ackroyd tries to unravel why she was being blackmailed and the truth of her blackmailer's identity, but he's stabbed to death in his study before he can find out. There are questions of inheritance, debt-ridden nieces and nephews, and an overly friendly neighborhood doctor who knows far too much. Muddy footprints outside the study where the murder took place, a missing Dictaphone, and a stranger at the train station all add to the mystery. Hercule Poirot is on the case interviewing them all (using his little grey cells) to find out what really went on at the estate of Fernly Park and who murdered Roger Ackroyd. This is one of Agatha's most controversial novels, as it breaks the mold of traditional mysteries and ends with an unexpected reveal!

4 ounces gin (I recommend Bar Hill)
1 ounce fresh lime juice
Club soda to top glasses
Mint sprigs, cucumber peels, and edible flowers for garnish

In a bar glass filled with ice, combine the gin and lime juice. Shake well (doctor's orders). Strain into ice-filled glasses. Top with club soda, garnish with mint sprigs, cucumber peels, and edible flowers, and serve.

Mocktail

Replace the gin with Seedlip Garden 28 or another nonalcoholic spirit.

ARTIST IN RESIDENCE

(Five Little Pigs)

---◆---

Serves 2

Hercule Poirot is visited by a young woman asking him to investigate her father's murder that took place sixteen years ago. Her mother, convicted of the crime, has sent a letter to her daughter from prison declaring her innocence. Hercule interviews the five people who were there on that fateful day (besides mother and daughter), dubbing them the five little pigs. Was it Amyas's best friend Philip Blake, the stockbroker; his best friend's older brother and Amyas's neighbor Meredith Blake; Caroline's younger stepsister Angela Warren; her stepsister's governess Cecelia Williams; or Amyas's painting model Elsa Greer, with whom he was having a scandalous affair? More importantly, which little piggy went wee, wee, wee, all the way home? Agatha's fascination with nursery rhymes is evident throughout her writing career. She thought them immensely entertaining and used them both in titles and themes.

2 ounces bourbon (I recommend Maker's Mark)

1 ounce ginger liqueur

1 ounce fresh lemon juice

1 ounce Honey Syrup (page 7)

6 ounces Belgian-style wheat beer to top glasses

Lemon twists for garnish

In a bar glass filled with ice, combine the bourbon, ginger liqueur, lemon juice, and Honey Syrup. Shake well and strain into glasses. Top with beer, garnish with a lemon twist, and serve.

Mocktail

Replace the bourbon with Kentucky 74 or another nonalcoholic bourbon, the ginger liqueur with 2 ounces Navy Hill or another ginger beer, and the Belgian-style wheat beer with any nonalcoholic beer such as Brooklyn Brewery Special Effects Hoppy Amber.

TRANSFUSION ON THE LINKS

(Murder on the Links)

---◆---

Serves 2

Hercule Poirot is called to France at the rushed bequest of a client. He arrives too late, as his client has been brutally stabbed and his body left in a shallow bunker on a golf course. Just as he begins gathering clues—a lead pipe, money deposited in a neighbor's bank account, and a disinherited son—a second murder occurs. Hercule's "little grey cells" take him to Paris to research a murder mystery that occurred more than twenty years before. He must sift through the clues that are par for the course and refrain from taking misguided swings to be sure his theory is a hole in one.

4 ounces vodka

4 ounces grape juice

3 ounces ginger beer

1 ounce fresh lime juice

Lime wheels for garnish

In a cocktail glass filled with ice, combine the vodka and grape and lime juices. Mix well. Strain into ice-filled glasses and top with ginger beer. Garnish with lime wheels and serve.

Mocktail

Replace the vodka with Optimist Botanicals Bright or another nonalcoholic spirit. Prepare as above.

ARLENA'S REVENGE

(Evil Under the Sun)

—— ◆ ——

Serves 2

Starlet Arlena Stuart Marshall is found dead on the private resort beach of the exclusive Jolly Roger Hotel in Devon, right down the road from where Hercule Poirot is enjoying his holiday. Intrigued, of course, he hesitates to come take a look at the case because the only way to get to the resort is by boat. (Hercule does not like boats.) But who killed Arlena? Loved by so many, hated by a select few, could it be the married man with an obvious deep infatuation, or his insanely jealous wife? Perhaps the murderer is Arlena's teenage stepdaughter who was staying with her but never really liked her at all. Was it a crime of passion or premeditated murder? Perhaps all that's needed for revenge is a delicious cocktail. Fun fact: The setting for this novel is actually the Art Deco–inspired Burgh Island Hotel and Resort off the coast of Devon, England, which hosts several murder mystery weekends during the course of the year. Dreamy interiors, music, beautiful scenery, and murder—what more could you want on your holiday?

1½ ounces scotch

   (I recommend Glenlivet Single Malt Scotch Whiskey)

2 ounces blood orange juice

1 ounce cherry brandy

1½ ounces sweet vermouth

Blood orange slices and luxardo cherries for garnish

In a shaker filled with ice, combine the scotch, blood orange juice, cherry brandy, and sweet vermouth. Shake well and strain into coupe glasses. Garnish with blood orange slices and luxardo cherries and serve.

Mocktail

Replace the scotch with Monday or another nonalcoholic spirit, the cherry brandy with cherry juice, and the sweet vermouth with Lyre's Aperitif Rosso or another nonalcoholic vermouth. Prepare as above. Garnish with maraschino cherries.

A IS FOR APEROL SPRITZ

(The ABC Murders)

Serves 2

There is a serial killer on the loose and Hercule Poirot, his companion Captain Arthur Hastings, and Chief Inspector Japp are on the case. Hercule is receiving letters from the killer signed "A.B.C." The murdered victims are piling up—Alice Ascher in Andover, Betty Barnard in Bexhill, Sir Carmichael Clarke in Churston—and panic is in the air. The killer leaves behind an ABC Rail Guide as a clue. Hercule has a theory, but the next murder occurs not in Doncaster like he thought. Could this throw off Hercule and his team of investigators? Or is the uncanny sleuth one letter ahead? The ABC Murders *is often considered to be Agatha's best novel.*

4 ounces aperol

6 ounces prosecco

2 ounces club soda

Orange slices for garnish

In two wineglasses filled halfway with ice, add the aperol, then the prosecco, and top with club soda. Stir twice, add orange slices for garnish, and serve.

Mocktail

Replace the aperol with Lyre's Italian Spritz or another nonalcoholic aperol and the prosecco with nonalcoholic sparkling brut champagne. Prepare as above.

B IS FOR BOULEVARDIER

(The ABC Murders)

— ◆ —

Serves 2

This popular variation of the classic negroni is dangerously drinkable and a perfect blend of sour, sweet, and bitter.

1½ ounces bourbon (I recommend Maker's Mark)

1 ounce Campari

1 ounce red sweet vermouth

Wide lemon peels for garnish

In a shaker filled with ice, combine all ingredients. Shake well and strain into rocks glasses over large ice cubes. Garnish with lemon peels and serve.

Mocktail

Replace the bourbon with Kentucky 74 or another nonalcoholic spirit, the Campari with Giffard Aperitif Syrup or another nonalcoholic aperitif, and the sweet vermouth with Blutul Rosso or another nonalcoholic vermouth. Prepare as above.

C IS FOR CAIPIRINHAS

(The ABC Murders)

Serves 2

1 lime, quartered
2 teaspoons white sugar or ¾ ounce Mint Simple Syrup
(page 6)
5 ounces Cachaça (Brazilian rum)

Add half the limes and sugar or Mint Simple Syrup to each glass and muddle. Add in 2½ ounces Cachaça and ice to each glass and stir. Garnish each glass with another lime wedge and serve.

Mocktail

Replace the Cachaça with Ritual Rum Alternative Zero Proof or another nonalcoholic spirit. Prepare as above.

GOLDEN HOUR

(A Caribbean Murder)

─────────── ◆ ───────────

Serves 2

All is not as it seems at the Golden Palm Resort on the Caribbean Island of St. Honoré. Miss Marple, one of Agatha's most enticing detectives, is set to enjoy her tropical respite at the lush resort until she gets trapped in a boring conversation with Major Palgrave about some murderer who got away with a crime long ago. The Major is found dead the next morning. The maid must've heard or seen something because she's the next victim in paradise. Miss Marple quickly finds herself in the middle of this tropical murder mystery. Sunny days melt into the extraordinary beauty of the golden hour before sunset, but in the darkness, she fears, danger looms. Could the murderer be on the island, and who will be his next victim? Let's mix up a cocktail that mimics the beautiful hue of golden hour, take our place in the shade, and observe the characters at hand to solve this crime.

> 6 ounces rum
>
>   (I recommend Montauk Rumrunners' Coconut Rum)
>
> 4 ounces pineapple juice
>
> 2 ounces orange juice
>
> 1 ounce lime juice
>
> Dark rum for floater, if desired
>
> Orange slices and pineapple wedges for garnish

In a shaker filled with ice, combine the rum and juices. Shake well and strain into ice-filled glasses. If desired, add a floater of dark rum to each glass. Garnish with pineapple wedges and orange slices and serve.

Mocktail

Replace the rum with Ritual Rum Alternative Zero Proof or another nonalcoholic spirit. Prepare as above.

AND THEN THERE WERE NEGRONIS

(And Then There Were None)

---◆---

Serves 2

Eight strangers, each with something to hide, are invited as weekend guests to an estate on a remote island off the English Coast. Their host? An eccentric millionaire unknown to them. When their host fails to appear, they begin questioning why they have been invited at all. With no way off the rugged island, they make the most of it over cocktails in the parlor and notice a sculpture set of ten figurines. When one of the party dies brutally by axe, they realize that there is a murderer among them, and one of the figurines is mysteriously missing! When the housekeeper falls dead in the kitchen from a lethal injection of potassium cyanide and another figurine goes missing, the group realizes why they were invited. Outrunning their past is no longer an option, and guilt, regret, and unpunished crimes can make people murder—again. A copy of the nursery rhyme "Ten Little Indians" is found, and when the group discovers that the murders are occurring as described in the rhyme, terror mounts. One by one they fall prey. Before the weekend is out, there will be none. Who has choreographed this villainous plot scheme? And who will be left to tell the tale? Only the dead are above suspicion. This is Agatha Christie's bestselling novel with more than one hundred million copies sold worldwide.

2 ounces gin (I recommend Bombay Sapphire)

2 ounces Campari

2 ounces sweet vermouth

Candied or torched orange peels for garnish

In a mixing glass over ice, combine the gin, Campari, and sweet vermouth. Strain into rocks glasses over large ice cubes. Express the oil from the orange peels over the drinks, then garnish and serve.

NEGRONI SBAGLIATO

(And Then There Were None)

Serves 2

3 ounces Campari

3 ounces sweet vermouth

3 ounces prosecco or sparkling wine

Candied or torched orange peels for garnish

In a mixing glass over ice, combine the Campari and sweet vermouth. Strain into rocks glasses over large ice cubes. Top with prosecco or sparkling wine. Express the oil from the orange peels over the drinks, then garnish and serve.

Mocktail

2 ounces gin (I recommend Monday)

2 ounces nonalcoholic Campari or red bitter liqueur
(I recommend Giffard Aperitif Syrup)

2 ounces nonalcoholic vermouth
(I recommend Lyre's Aperitif Rosso)

1 dropper nonalcoholic orange bitters
(I recommend All The Bitter Orange Bitters)

1 dropper nonalcoholic bitters
(I recommend All The Bitter Aromatic Bitters)

Candied or torched orange peels for garnish

Add all ingredients to a mixing glass with ice. Stir and strain into rocks glasses over large ice cubes. Express the oil from the orange peels over the drinks, then garnish and serve.

THE MINTED MAN

(The Man in the Brown Suit)

———— ◆ ————

Serves 2

Anne Beddingfield, a young woman recently orphaned, has come to London seeking adventure. Waiting for the tube at Hyde Park Corner, she watches a man fall off the platform, electrocuted by the live rails. Another man in a brown suit examines him, claiming to be a doctor, then runs off, leaving a paper behind. When Anne picks it up, it reads "17.1 22 Kilmorden Castle." Perplexed, Anne is determined to find out who this man is and what he has to do with the tube station death. After learning that Kilmorden is a luxury cruise ship bound for South Africa, Anne books a ticket and sets sail. As she dives deeper into her adventure, she survives an attempt on her life and learns of missing diamonds that multiple people would kill to find. The crushed ice in this classic cocktail shines bright like the missing diamonds Anne is determined to find.

> 10 mint leaves, plus sprigs for garnish
> 1 ounce Mint Simple Syrup (page 6)
> 4 ounces bourbon (I recommend Maker's Mark)
> Crushed ice
> 3 dashes angostura bitters

Lightly slapping the mint leaves against the back of your palm will help release their oils and scent and make the mint more aromatic. In julep cups, muddle the mint leaves and Mint Simple Syrup. Add the bourbon between both cups, fill cups with crushed ice, and stir until glasses are frosty. Top with more crushed ice, add in the bitters, and garnish with mint sprigs. Serve.

Mocktail

Replace the bourbon with Kentucky 74 or another nonalcoholic spirit and the bitters with All The Bitter New Orleans or other nonalcoholic bitters. Prepare as above.

MESOPOTAMIA MAI TAI

(Murder in Mesopotamia)

◆

Serves 2

In the Iraqi desert at an ancient archeological site, Nurse Amy Leatheran is tending to the head archaeologist's wife, Louise, who is suffering from neurotic episodes. When Louise winds up dead, Amy thinks there is something devious going on. Thankfully, Hercule Poirot is on his way! Can he help dig out the truth behind what seems to be murder? Some of the characters in this book were inspired by Agatha's own travels with husband Sir Max Mallowan on archaeological digs.

> 2 ounces rum
> (I recommend Montauk Rumrunners' Coconut Rum)
> 1 ounce Curaçao or grand marnier
> ½ ounce orgeat syrup
> 6 ounces pineapple juice
> 1½ ounces lime juice
> 2 ounces spiced dark rum for floater, if desired
> (I recommend Plantation)
> Lime wheels and pineapple spears for garnish

In a shaker filled with ice, combine the rum, Curaçao or grand marnier, orgeat syrup, and juices. Shake well and strain into ice-filled glasses. If desired, add a floater of dark rum to each glass. Garnish with lime wheels and pineapple spears and serve.

Mocktail

Replace both rums with Ritual Rum Alternative Zero Proof or another nonalcoholic spirit, and the Curaçao or grand marnier with 1 ounce coconut cream and 1 ounce fresh orange juice. Prepare as above.

PIMM'S AT POLLENSA BAY

(Problem at Pollensa Bay)

◆

Serves 2

Parker Pyne is desperate for a relaxing respite. He is just settling into his stay at the luxurious Hotel Pino d'Oro on Pollensa Bay on the island of Mallorca when he is approached by another British guest asking him for his assistance in discouraging her son from going ahead with a less than desirable marriage. This story is an ode to the lighter side of Agatha's writing, and part of a collection of short stories featuring one of her classic characters, Parker Pyne. Insisting that he is not a detective, this chubby, older gentleman is on a quest in his second career to cure unhappiness. Let's raise a glass to that! Fun fact: Hotel Pino d'Oro is said to be fashioned after the Hotel Illa d'Or, where Agatha stayed on vacation in March of 1932.

4 ounces Pimm's No. 1

1 ounce lemon juice

6 ounces sparkling lemonade

Cucumber, lemon, and orange slices, strawberries,
    and basil for garnish

Powdered sugar to top glasses

Fill two glasses with ice, then divide the Pimm's No. 1 and lemon juice between them. Stir and divide the sparkling lemonade between each glass. Garnish with sliced cucumber, lemon, and orange, strawberries, and basil. Dust with powdered sugar, if desired. Serve.

Mocktail

Replace Pimm's No. 1 with ANON English Garden or another nonalcoholic spirit. Prepare as above.

MATCH POINT

(Towards Zero)

◆

Serves 2 (why play singles when you can play doubles?)

A house party gathers at Gull's Point in the lovely seaside home of Lady Tressilian. Among the guests are a famous tennis star, his former wife, and his current wife (and this is a good idea because . . . ?) What a racquet! *During dinner, a family friend tells the true story of a child killing another child with an arrow. After it was ruled an accident, the child was given a new identity and relocated. The next morning, the family friend is found dead. (40-love). Soon after, Lady Tressilian is found in her bed, bludgeoned to death (ad-out), her maid drugged and unconscious (game, set, match). Superintendent Battle is called in to find out who is behind these killings. But to do so, he'll need a strong serve.*

3 ounces vodka

6 ounces lemonade

2 ounces passion fruit nectar

1 ounce elderflower liqueur (I recommend Heimat)

Melon balls, mint sprigs, and edible flowers for garnish

In a shaker filled with ice, combine the vodka, lemonade, passion fruit nectar, and elderflower liqueur. Shake well and strain into ice-filled glasses. Garnish with melon balls, mint sprigs, and edible flowers. *Serve!*

Mocktail

Replace the vodka with Seedlip Spice 94 or another nonalcoholic spirit and the elderflower liqueur with fresh raspberry or pomegranate juice. Prepare as above.

MEWS HOUSE PARTY PUNCH

(Murder in the Mews)

———— ◆ ————

Serves 2

Inspector Japp asks Hercule Poirot to take a look at an investigative scene. A young lady appears to have committed suicide at her house in the Mews. But to this dynamic duo of crime solvers, something seems off. Hercule wonders why a young woman who is right-handed would have a wound above her left ear. Is this a murder meant to look like a suicide . . . or a suicide meant to look like a murder? With no apparent motive or suicide note, Hercule must use his "little grey cells" to find the answers. This refreshing cocktail has a mix of sweet, tart, earthy, and bubbly layers—all distinct, much like Agatha's characters in this entertaining novel.

> 2 ounces cherry juice
> 1 ounce lime juice
> 1 ounce Honey Syrup (page 7)
> 3 ounces white rum (I recommend Plantation)
> Chilled prosecco to top glasses (I recommend La Marca)
> Thyme sprigs and cherries for garnish

In a bar glass, combine the cherry and lime juices and Honey Syrup. Pour in the rum, add ice, and shake. Strain into glasses and top with prosecco. Garnish with thyme sprigs and cherries and serve.

Mocktail

Replace the rum with Ritual Rum Alternative Zero Proof or another nonalcoholic spirit and the prosecco with Wölffer Estate Spring in a Bottle or another nonalcoholic prosecco. Prepare as above.

GARDEN PARTIES, STOLEN IDENTITIES & UNSCRUPULOUS VICARS

Gardens gave Agatha great joy, especially the gardens at Greenway, her beloved holiday home. There with its beautiful walled gardens, camelia garden, greenhouse, and riverside woodlands that lead down to the boathouse, she would relax and enjoy her family time. Her boathouse was featured in *Dead Man's Folly*, and across the river in Battery is where *Five Little Pigs* was set. As a child, Agatha spent time with imaginary friends, thus wielding an extraordinary imagination. She was a fine listener, spending more time observing than speaking. She once said, "I usually have about half a dozen [notebooks] on hand and I used to make notes in them of clever ideas that struck me, or about some person or drug, or a clever little bit of swindling that I had read about in the paper." She appreciated the daily life and buzz of English villages and towns and wrote frequently about the goings on, the gossip, and the vicarages. To Agatha, nothing was mundane.

MOCKTAILS & MURDER

◆

Serves 2

Agatha's passion for exotic locations and adventure set the scenes for many of her stories. She traveled frequently to Egypt, France, and Morocco with her second husband, prominent British archeologist Sir Max Mallowan, and brought these fascinating (and culturally striking) locales and experiences to her writing. At home, she relished time on her English estate, Styles, where she loved to look out upon the gardens while writing. Agatha was not one to partake in cocktails, so this mocktail is a perfect fresh-from-the-garden combination of all-natural spices and flavors that she might have enjoyed.

4 ounces nonalcoholic spirit (I recommend Seedlip Grove 42)

2 ounces Rhubarb Syrup (page 6)

6 drops nonalcoholic bitters (I recommend All The Bitter)

Club soda to top glasses

Rhubarb ribbons for garnish

In a shaker filled with ice, combine the nonalcoholic spirit, Rhubarb Syrup, and bitters. Shake well and strain into ice-filled glasses. Top with club soda, garnish with a rhubarb ribbon, and serve.

THE CONFESSION

(Murder at the Vicarage)

◆

Serves 2

In the village of St. Mary Mead, the vicarage is buzzing over dinner when the clergyman shares that getting rid of or perhaps even killing Colonel Protheroe would be a welcome occurrence. Everyone around the table chimes in agreement and shares exactly how they would "off" him. (Apparently, no one is a fan!) When the Colonel is found shot to death in the vicar's study the next day, heads begin to roll in this sleepy village. It's a good thing Miss Marple, who happens to live next door to the vicarage, sees the comings and goings of everyone from her window. As suspects are questioned—the colonel's widow and her lover, his nephews, the vicar's young, flirty wife, and the colonel's daughter, who couldn't stand her controlling father—it becomes apparent that there is more than meets the eye over the garden walls. Someone better start confessing!

2 ounces sake

2 ounces raspberry liqueur (I recommend Heimat)

1½ ounces limoncello

4 ounces peach nectar

1 ounce fresh lemon juice

Champagne to top glasses

In a shaker filled with ice, combine all ingredients except the champagne. Shake and strain, praying that it's nice and cold. Divide evenly between flute glasses, filling halfway, and top with champagne. Serve.

Mocktail

Replace the champagne with Wölffer Estate Spring in a Bottle or another nonalcoholic champagne, the sake with Gekkeiken alcohol-free Daiginjo Sake or another nonalcoholic sake, the raspberry liqueur with Stonewall Kitchen raspberry syrup or another nonalcoholic raspberry syrup, and the limoncello with Lemon Simple Syrup (page 8). Prepare as above.

"What are you doing this afternoon, Griselda?"

"My duty as the Vicaress. Tea and scandal at four-thirty."

—Agatha Christie, *Murder at the Vicarage*

BLACK MAGIC

(The Pale Horse)

— ◆ —

Serves 2

What could a list of names, a murdered clergyman, and the sinister workings of black magic have in common? According to Mark Easterbrook, this story's dashing main character, clearly something. Bringing his sidekick Ginger along, Mark launches his own witch hunt into the names on the list and their respective murders. He discovers that they are somehow tied to the Pale Horse Inn. Going right to the source, he visits the Pale Horse Inn and begins to immerse himself in the world of witchcraft, love potions, and death potions. Will Mark be able to string clues together before his own name is added to the list? Let's hope so. In the meantime, mix up this cocktail that's sure to cast the right kind of spell! Fun fact: The title of this book comes from Revelation 6:8: "And I looked, and behold a pale horse: and his name that sat on him was Death, and Hell followed with him."

6 ounces red wine (I recommend pinot noir)

1½ ounces grand marnier

3 ounces pomegranate juice

1 ounce Winter Spice Syrup (page 7)

Orange wheels and mint sprigs for garnish

In a shaker filled with ice, combine all ingredients. Shake well (to release any evil spirits) and strain into glasses. Garnish with orange wheels and mint sprigs. Serve.

Mocktail

Replace the red wine with Waterbrook Clean red wine or another non-alcoholic wine and the grand marnier with Lyre's Italian Orange or another nonalcoholic aperitif. Prepare as above.

THE LOBBY

(At Bertram's Hotel)

---◆---

Servess 2

Bertram's Hotel, frequented by aristocrats and the well-to-do, has sentimental meaning for Miss Marple. She stayed here as a child on holiday, but her stay this time around is nothing like a holiday, as she encounters a wave of criminal activity. The Irish Mail train has been robbed, there are death threats, and cold-blooded murder, all surrounded by fast getaway cars and jewel heists. No one is who they seem. Can't Miss Marple have a relaxing vacation? Apparently not, as the very hotel is being used as a cover for a criminal ring! Time to head straight to the lobby bar for a batch of these delightful cocktails. The Fleming's Mayfair, one of the hotels thought to be the inspiration behind Bertram's Hotel, features several cocktails named in Dame Agatha's honor. If I could add one cocktail to their repertoire, this would be the one. The pear liqueur gives it a jolt of flavor, much like Miss Marple.

> 4 ounces blanco tequila (I recommend Casamigos)
>
> 2 ounces pear liqueur
> > (I recommend Heimat Barrel Finished Bosc Pear Liqueur)
>
> 2 ounces pear nectar
>
> 1 ounce Winter Spice Syrup (page 7)
>
> 1 ounce lime juice
>
> Pear slices and whole nutmeg, grated, for garnish

In a shaker filled with ice, combine all ingredients. Shake well and strain into ice-filled glasses. Garnish with pear slices and grated nutmeg on top. Serve.

Mocktail

Replace the tequila with ISH Mexican Agave Spirit or another nonalcoholic spirit and the pear liqueur with Monin Pear Syrup or another pear syrup. Prepare as above.

FOLLY FROSÉ

(Dead Man's Folly)

———————— ◆ ————————

Serves 2

Who knew hosting a garden party could be so deadly? A mock murder game has been organized at the home of Sir George and Lady Stubbs, the hosts of a village summer fete. They hire Miss Adriadne Oliver, a well-known crime writer, to organize the fun. Despite weeks of meticulous planning, an impeding sense of danger grasps Adriadne, and she calls her friend Hercule Poirot to come and calm her suspicions. But disaster looms, and on the day of the murder mystery the girl playing the dead girl is found dead in the boathouse. This sets off a series of events that include strange impersonations, wives from past lives, and a missing fortune. Who would be fool enough to get away with it? Let's sit back, enjoy this garden-inspired libation, and examine the clues. Two sleuths are better than one!

2 cups rosé
1 cup frozen peaches
2 ounces gin (I recommend Wölffer)
2 ounces nectarine liqueur (I recommend Heimat Nectarine)
Fresh nectarine or peach slices for garnish

In a blender, add the rosé, frozen peaches, gin, and liqueur. Add 1 cup ice. Blend until smooth. Pour into glasses, garnish with nectarine or peach slices, and serve.

Mocktail

Replace the rosé with Wölffer Estate Spring in a Bottle or another nonalcoholic wine, the gin with Seedlip Grove 42 or another nonalcoholic spirit, and the nectarine liqueur with Ceres Peach Nectar.

PALOMA AT END HOUSE

(Peril at End House)

---◆---

Serves 2

Hercule Poirot and his companion Captain Arthur Hastings are on holiday when they run into a curious young woman, Nick Buckley, who believes her life is in danger. (After all, a girl who survives failed brakes down a Cornish hillside, a boulder dropped toward her on a coastal path, and a bullet shot straight through her sun hat that escapes her altogether, should seriously look into protection.) Alas, the Belgian sleuth cannot help but become engrossed in her misfortunes. After Nick's cousin comes to visit and is killed, a love triangle comes to the surface along with a timely drug addiction and a forged will. Is it happy hour yet?

Coarse sea salt to rim glasses

Lime wheels, plus extra for garnish

4 ounces tequila (I recommend Casamigos)

4 ounces fresh grapefruit juice

1 ounce lime juice

4 dashes bitters
   (I recommend Mister Bitters Pink Grapefruit & Agave)

Grapefruit soda to top glasses

Grapefruit wedges for garnish

Rim two glasses with coarse sea salt by pouring salt in a shallow dish, rubbing each rim with a slice of lime, and turning the glass rims in the salt until coated. Let set. In a shaker filled with ice, combine the tequila, grapefruit and lime juices, and bitters. Shake well and divide into ice-filled glasses. Top with grapefruit soda and garnish with lime wheels. Serve.

Mocktail

Replace the tequila with ISH Mexican Agave Spirit or another non-alcoholic spirit and the bitters with El Guapo Fuego Bitters or other nonalcoholic bitters. Prepare as above.

SEASIDE SANGRIA

(Sleeping Murder)

◆

Serves 6

Gwenda Reed, a wealthy young newlywed recently emigrated from India, impulsively buys a seaside manor with grand plans to renovate it into the home of her dreams. As her renovations are underway, she starts having flashbacks of her past life. First, a hidden room is discovered with the same wallpaper she had been dreaming of. Then, a line from a play makes her scream in fright! Out of fear, she turns to Miss Marple to help her find out what ghosts from the past might destroy her future. Fun fact: this was Agatha's last published novel.

> 1 (750-milliliter) bottle red wine
>
> (I recommend rioja, grenache, or California red blend)
>
> 4 ounces cranberry liqueur
>
> (I recommend Heimat Cranberry)
>
> 4 ounces brandy
>
> 4 ounces lemonade
>
> 4 ounces orange juice
>
> Orange wheels and fresh strawberries
>
> 12 ounces sparkling water

In a pitcher, combine all ingredients except the sparkling water. Let the flavors marry for up to thirty minutes. Add ice and top with sparkling water. Serve.

Mocktail

Replace the red wine with Sovi Red Blend or another nonalcoholic wine, the cranberry liqueur with cranberry juice, and the brandy with Lyre's Italian Orange or another nonalcoholic aperitif.

"Out flew the web
and floated wide;

The mirror crack'd
from side to side;

'The curse is come
upon me,' cried

The Lady of Shalott."

—Alfred, Lord Tennyson,
"The Lady of Shalot"

MIRROR CRACK'D FROM SIDE TO SIDECAR

(The Mirror Crack'd from Side to Side)

---◆---

Serves 2

Hollywood comes to St. Mary Mead, a proper English village that is home to the one and only Miss Marple, forever changing the landscape and look of the village. Miss Marple is not a fan. At a summer fete hosted by the glamorous Marina Gregg and her husband Jason, nosy neighbor Heather Badcock begins chatting away with the star, telling her what a huge fan she is and that she saw her years ago in Bermuda, when suddenly Heather suffers a seizure and dies. Traces of poison were found in Marina's daiquiri. The plot thickens as it is discovered that both Heather and Marina were drinking daiquiris—for whom the poison was intended. Miss Marple learns that some amounts of suffering and heartbreak can be endured, but too much can make one crack from side to side.

> 4 ounces VSOP cognac, Armagnac, or good California brandy
>
> 2 ounces grand marnier
>
> 1½ ounces lemon juice
>
> Orange twists for garnish

In a shaker, combine the cognac, Armagnac, or good California brandy, grand marnier, and lemon juice. Add ice and shake well. Strain over large ice cubes into rocks glasses. Garnish with orange twists and serve.

Mocktail

Replace the cognac, Armagnac, or good California brandy with ArKay Non-Alcoholic Brandy or another nonalcoholic spirit and the grand marnier with Lyre's Italian Orange or another nonalcoholic aperitif. Prepare as above.

BLACKBERRY MARTINI

(Hallowe'en Party)

Serves 2

During a teenage Halloween party in Woodleigh Common, thirteen-year-old Joyce Reynolds boasts to everyone that she once witnessed a murder. Not sharing any of the details, no one there believes her, and proceeds to make fun of her seemingly tall tale. As the party ends, Joyce is found dead, drowned in the apple bobbing barrel, her bumblebee costume dripping on the floor. Adriadne Oliver, who was at the party visiting her friend, calls Hercule Poirot to investigate the murder and the evil presence lurking about. As Hercule begins his investigation, he finds that there are several past deaths and disappearances in Woodleigh Common that don't add up. As the world's most famous detective bobs for clues, he must work with Adriadne and her intuition to stop the haunting.

> 4 ounces vodka (I recommend Belvedere)
> 1½ ounces blackberry liqueur (I recommend Heimat New York Blackberry)
> 1 ounce Blackberry-Hibiscus Simple Syrup (page 9)
> 1 ounce fresh lemon juice
> 3 dashes bitters (I recommend All The Bitters New Orleans)
> Blackberries, lemon peels, and mint sprigs for garnish

In a shaker filled with ice, combine the vodka, blackberry liqueur, Blackberry-Hibiscus Simple Syrup, and lemon juice. Shake until the evil presence has gone and the cocktail is well-chilled. Strain into martini glasses and garnish with blackberries, lemon peels, and mint sprigs. Serve.

Mocktail

Replace the vodka with Monday or another nonalcoholic spirit and the blackberry liqueur with white cranberry juice. Prepare as above.

TRAINS, PLANES & MURDERS ON THE GO

Agatha's love for adventure took her to places where she could revel in nature, cultures, history, and landscapes. Not one to be idle, she was always hopping a train, plane, or auto and so her novels are often set in these modes of transport that she experienced and relished.

ORIENT ESPRESSO MARTINI

(Murder on the Orient Express)

◆

Serves 2

Murder on the Orient Express is undoubtedly one of Agatha's most famous novels. Long obsessed with the magnificence of the Orient Express, a most luxurious train, Agatha infuses glorious detail of the train's décor throughout her book. The story creates an intimate look at thirteen strangers trapped on the Orient Express as it encounters a snowstorm while traveling through the Balkans. The infamous Hercule Poirot, who happens to be traveling on the same train, discovers that one of the passengers has been bludgeoned to death in their stateroom. Now, with a murderer among them, the famous detective must use his "little grey cells" to solve the crime and identify the murderer before he or she strikes again. Quite a glamorous setting for a murder mystery, the opulent train stuck in a snowdrift is an enthrallingly beautiful visual. This delectable cocktail is perfect to keep you warm, alert, and on guard until the murderer is revealed.

4 ounces vodka

1 ounce Kahlúa

2 ounces espresso

½ ounce Basic Simple Syrup (page 6)

Star anise or espresso beans for garnish

In a shaker filled with ice, combine all ingredients and shake until frothy. Strain into martini glasses and garnish each cocktail with a star anise or espresso beans. Serve.

Mocktail

Replace the vodka with Monday or another nonalcoholic spirit, and the Kahlúa with DaVinci Gourmet Coffee or another coffee-flavored syrup. Prepare as above.

SNOWDRIFT SCANDAL

(Murder on the Orient Express)

◆

Serves 2

The 2017 film adaptation of Murder on the Orient Express *stars British actor Kenneth Branagh as Hercule Poirot along with Johnny Depp, Michelle Pfeiffer, Judi Dench, and Leslie Odom Jr. as part of an award-winning ensemble cast. The stunningly rich interiors and wardrobe are reasons enough to watch, as they celebrate the golden age of travel and Agatha's timeless novel. Here's to enjoying a cocktail as rich as this film. Magnificent, grand, luxurious, lavishly detailed, and period perfect.*

> 3 ounces brandy
>
> 2 ounces rum (I recommend Plantation)
>
> ½ ounce orange liqueur (I recommend Orange Curaçao)
>
> 1½ ounces fresh lemon juice
>
> ½ ounce Basic Simple Syrup (page 6)
>
> Club soda to top glasses
>
> Orange peels for garnish

In a shaker, combine all ingredients except club soda. Add ice and shake until well-chilled. Strain into glasses. Top each glass with club soda, garnish with an orange peel, and serve.

Mocktail

Replace the brandy with ArKay Non-Alcoholic Brandy or another non-alcoholic spirit, the rum with Ritual Rum Alternative Zero Proof or another nonalcoholic spirit, and the orange liqueur with Lyre's Italian Orange or another nonalcoholic aperitif. Prepare as above.

DISAPPEARING ACT

◆

Serves 2

On a cold December night in 1926, Agatha took a drive, telling her secretary that she'd be away for the night, and disappeared for eleven days. The search took on a dramatic mystery of its own with hundreds of policemen and locals playing sleuth trying to find her with few clues: Her car on the edge of a pond and her fur coat slung over the back seat. She was eventually found at an upscale hotel/spa in Yorkshire, having checked in under her then-husband's mistress's name. Agatha cited amnesia as the reason for her disappearance, resulting from hitting her head when her car crashed into brush. There are many unanswered questions, but could the Maiden of Murder have outsmarted both the authorities and amateur sleuths alike, creating the most famous mystery of all? Either way, Agatha was returned home safe and sound and her book sales went soaring. Let's raise our glasses to that!

4 ounces gin (I recommend Wölffer)

2 ounces peach nectar

½ ounce nectarine liqueur (I recommend Heimat Nectarine)

1 ounce fresh lemon juice

Prosecco to top glasses

Edible flowers for garnish

In a shaker filled with ice, combine the gin, peach nectar, nectarine liqueur, and lemon juice. Shake well and strain into glasses. Top with prosecco, garnish with edible flowers, and serve. Cheers to always finding your way home!

Mocktail

Replace the gin with Roots Divino or another nonalcoholic gin, nectarine liqueur with more peach nectar, and prosecco with Gruvi or another nonalcoholic prosecco. Prepare as above.

DAIQUIRI ON THE NILE

(Death on the Nile)

---◆---

Serves 2

The romance and splendor of Hercule Poirot's luxury cruise along the Nile is shattered by the murder of a beautiful young woman, shot to death in her stateroom. How can such evil lurk in a land of magnificent beauty? Mourning her death is her newlywed husband, her cousin who is also her solicitor (and also stealing funds), and an old lover, a doctor, who is still madly in love with her. But Hercule quickly realizes, everyone on board has a motive. As dead bodies pile up like bricks in the ancient temple of Ramses II, the rich story lines keep you entertained, on edge, and guessing until the grand reveal. Let's mix a cocktail and retire to the sun lounge while listening to fabulous jazz music—cocktail in hand!

> 4 ounces light rum (I recommend Plantation)
> 2 ounces fresh lime juice
> 1 ounce Basic Simple Syrup (page 6)
> Lime twists for garnish

In a shaker filled with ice, combine all ingredients. Shake well and strain into coupe glasses. Garnish each glass with a lime twist and serve.

Mocktail

Replace the rum with Seedlip Garden 108 or another nonalcoholic spirit. Prepare as above.

"It is always the facts that do not fit in that are significant."

—Agatha Christie, *Death on the Nile*

EGYPTIAN JEWEL

(Death on the Nile)

---◆---

Serves 2

One of Agatha's most beloved novels and a Hollywood favorite, Death on the Nile *has been adapted for film three times, most recently in 2022 with Kenneth Branagh returning as Hercule Poirot, Tom Bateman as Bouc, and an ensemble cast that includes Armie Hammer, Gal Gadot, Annette Bening, Russell Brand, and Sophie Okonedo. Masterfully directed and produced, one is immediately taken away into an exotic setting of love, jealousy, and betrayal. The moving plotlines are only outdone by the shifting sands and red carmine Egyptian sunsets.*

    2 ounces cranberry liqueur (I recommend Heimat Cranberry)
    2 ounces cherry juice
    ½ ounce lemon juice
    Prosecco to top glasses

In a small pitcher, combine the liqueur and juices. Chill in the refrigerator for up to one hour. Pour mixture into flute glasses, top with prosecco, and serve.

Mocktail

Replace the prosecco with Chateau de Fleur or another nonalcoholic sparkling wine and the cranberry liqueur with cranberry juice. Prepare as above.

DESTINATION MOJITO

(Destination Unknown)

———— ◆ ————

Serves 2

When several leading scientists go missing without a trace, the international intelligence committee takes notice. As a young woman loses her zest for life and plots her own suicide, a man introduces himself with an offer of a much better way to die: To partake in the mission to find these scientists by stealing someone else's identity. Hilary accepts his offer and finds herself heading to the Atlas Mountains in Morocco to a secret research facility. Could Hilary find adventure, a new outlook on life, all while falling in love with a scientist she's trying to save? Let's mix a batch of this cocktail before unpacking it all.

10 mint leaves, plus extra for garnish

1½ ounces lime juice

1 ounce Honey Syrup (page 7)

4 ounces white rum (I recommend Plantation)

Club soda to top glasses

Lime wheels for garnish

In each glass, muddle 5 mint leaves, ¾ ounce lime juice, and ½ ounce Honey Syrup. Add in 2 ounces rum to each glass and stir. Fill glasses with crushed ice and top with club soda. Garnish with more mint leaves and lime wheels and serve.

Mocktail

Replace the rum with Ritual Rum Alternative Zero Proof or another nonalcoholic spirit. Prepare as above.

4:50 FOR A BLOOD ORANGE OLD FASHIONED

(4:50 from Paddington)

Serve 2

When another train comes up alongside Elspeth's train window, she sees a man strangle a woman to death. After relaying the story to her friend Miss Marple, the quest is on to find the body, any witnesses, and the murderer. With limited police help, these ladies have to find their inner superpower to solve the crime, starting by riding the train to see where the body might've been discarded. This novel has more twists and turns than a jagged track, so hold on to your cocktail because this train is about to leave the station. Miss Marple must build the case just like this delicious cocktail—from scratch.

> 4 ounces bourbon
>
> (I recommend Maker's Mark or Michter's US1)
>
> 4 ounces blood orange juice
>
> 4 dashes aromatic bitters
>
> ½ ounce Honey Rosemary Simple Syrup (page 9)
>
> Blood orange slices for garnish

In a shaker filled with ice, combine all ingredients and stir three times to marry flavors. Strain into glasses, garnish with blood orange slices, and serve.

Mocktail

Replace the bourbon with Kentucky 74 or another nonalcoholic spirit and the bitters with All The Bitters Orange Bitters or other nonalcoholic bitters. Prepare as above.

AVIATION

(Death in the Clouds)

⸻ ◆ ⸻

Serve 2

In this classic locked-room mystery, Hercule Poirot is enjoying his flight from London to Paris in seat No. 9, observing (as he does) the people around him. In seat No. 13 is a countess with a poorly concealed cocaine habit, in seat No. 8 is a detective writer swatting an annoying wasp, and a few rows ahead is a young woman flirting overtly with the man directly opposite her. What he doesn't see is a woman in seat No. 2 get struck and killed by a poisoned dart during the flight. Hercule, sometimes with his head in the clouds, must use his "little grey cells" to uncover the truth. This cocktail is perfect jet fuel for the mission. Agatha was a huge fan of air travel and described flying as extraordinary.

4 ounces gin (I recommend Aviation American)

½ ounce crème de violette

1 ounce maraschino liqueur

1 ounce lemon juice

In a shaker filled with ice, combine all ingredients. With your tray table in an upright, locked position, shake well and strain into coupe glasses. Garnish with brandied cherries or lemon peels and serve.

Mocktail

Replace the gin with Monday or another nonalcoholic spirit, the crème de violette with Épicerie de Provence Violet Syrup or another violet syrup, and the maraschino liqueur with fresh cherry juice. Prepare as above.

LE TRAIN BLEU

(The Mystery of the Blue Train)

◆

Serve 2

Aboard the luxurious Blue Train traveling from London to the French Riviera, a young American heiress on the way to meet her lover is murdered, her priceless rubies stolen. Coincidentally, her estranged husband is on the same train with his mistress. Thankfully, Hercule Poirot is also aboard to help solve this classic mystery filled with passion, greed, deceit, and, of course, murder. All aboard! The Blue Train, or Le Train Bleu, named for its deep blue sleeping cars, was an actual French luxury night train that ran from 1886–2003. It gained international fame as the preferred train of the rich and famous.

> 4 ounces gin (I recommend Bombay Sapphire)
> 1½ ounces Cointreau
> 1 ounce Curaçao
> 1½ ounces lemon juice
> Orange peels for garnish

In a shaker filled with ice, combine all ingredients. Shake well and strain into champagne or coupe glasses. Garnish with orange peels and serve.

Mocktail

Replace the gin with Monday or another nonalcoholic spirit, the Cointreau with Monin Triple Sec Syrup or similar syrup, and the Curaçao with Torani Blue Curaçao Syrup or similar syrup. Prepare as above.

FRENCH 75 TO FRANKFURT

(Passenger to Frankfurt)

◆

Serve 2

Diplomat Sir Stafford Nye's journey home to London takes an unexpected twist in the passenger lounge at Frankfurt Airport when a young woman confides in him that someone is trying to kill her. Nye hesitantly lends this mysterious woman his passport and quickly finds himself in a web of international espionage and danger, his life in serious jeopardy. Cocktail, anyone? Enter the French 75, a cocktail that can go anywhere and is discreet enough to go undercover and hide in plain sight. Cognac is called for instead of gin as a nod to its original French origins, but also because a spy is never what they seem. It's always a good idea to add a bit of intrigue to your cocktails too. This was Agatha's eightieth book, published in tandem with her eightieth birthday.

2 ounces cognac
2 ounces Basic Simple Syrup (page 6)
1½ ounces lemon juice
Chilled brut champagne to top glasses
Lemon twists for garnish

In a shaker filled with ice, combine the cognac, Basic Simple Syrup, and lemon juice. Shake until well-chilled (or you realize giving your passport to a stranger is *not* a good idea). Divide the mixture between flute glasses and top with chilled champagne. Garnish with lemon twists and serve.

Mocktail

Replace the champagne with Chateau de Fleur or another nonalcoholic sparkling wine and the cognac with ArKay Non-Alcoholic Brandy or another nonalcoholic spirit. Prepare as above.

FAMILY DYNAMICS & DEADLY DISTURBANCES

F amily dynamics are one of Agatha's main themes throughout her writing. Coming from a small family of modest means, it's ironic that she wrote so freely about multigenerational families living under the same roof, often in grand family estates. Her stories masterfully expose her characters' evil tendencies or capacities, especially if there's a will to be read and inheritance to be gained, ultimately proving that the grass isn't always greener behind those iron gates—sometimes it's deadly.

CORPSE REVIVER NO. 2

(After the Funeral)

Serve 2

Wealthy Richard Abernethie dies suddenly, and his estranged sister Cora is convinced it's murder. But when Cora is murdered the next day, the family solicitor hires Hercule Poirot to find Cora's killer and solve the mystery of Richard's death. As Hercule makes himself part of the family, watching everyone's moves and listening to their conversations, he realizes that people are not at all who they seem and is certain that the murderer, through actions or lies, will reveal themselves.

- 2 ounces gin (I recommend Aviation American)
- 2 ounces Lillet Blanc
- 2 ounces Cointreau
- 2 ounces lemon juice
- 2 dashes absinthe

In a shaker filled with ice, combine all ingredients and shake until well-chilled. Strain into chilled glasses and serve.

Mocktail

Replace Lillet Blanc with Blutul Bianco Vermouth or another nonalcoholic vermouth, the Cointreau with Lyre's Italian Orange or another nonalcoholic aperitif, the gin with Monday or another nonalcoholic spirit, and the absinthe with Lyre's Non-Alcoholic Absinthe or another nonalcoholic absinthe. Prepare as above.

A VIEW FROM THE TREEHOUSE

(Crooked House)

◆

Serve 2

Agatha once said that Crooked House *was one of her best works. When wealthy Greek businessman Aristide Leonides is found poisoned to death at Three Gables, his sprawling mansion in the suburbs of London, his widow, Brenda, fifty years his junior, is a prime suspect. She's set to inherit a large sum and rumored to be carrying on a torrid affair with the live-in tutor. Scandalously fabulous! Sophia, the late millionaire's granddaughter, hires criminologist and ex-fiancé Charles Hayward to solve the crime. Charles knows the Leonides family well and is certain that, in this crooked house, one of them is not level. But to Charles, pinning this crime on Brenda seems too easy. As Charles takes a closer look through the treehouse window, things begin to become a bit clearer, but no one is ready for the reveal. This delicate cocktail has a surprisingly refreshing taste: Transparent, unlike the many characters in this crooked house.*

> 4 ounces fresh sugar snap peas or English garden peas,
>   plus extra for garnish
> 1 ounce fresh lemon juice
> 1 ounce Tarragon Simple Syrup (page 8)
> 1 ounce dry vermouth
> 4 ounces vodka

In a shaker, muddle the peas, lemon juice, and Tarragon Simple Syrup. Add in the vermouth and vodka, then fill the shaker with ice and shake until chilled. Strain into coupe glasses, garnish with snap peas, and serve.

Mocktail

Replace the vodka with Monday or another nonalcoholic spirit and the vermouth with Blutul Bianco Vermouth or another nonalcoholic vermouth. Prepare as above.

DEATH BY THE DEAD SEA

(Appointment with Death)

◆

Serve 2

On holiday in Jerusalem, Hercule Poirot overhears Raymond Boyton tell his sister, "You do see, don't you, that she's got to be killed?" They were, of course, talking about their stepmother. Mrs. Boynton is a perverse tyrant who dominates her family. When she is found dead on an excursion to Petra, Hercule wonders if her stepchildren, desperate to live their own lives, would kill for freedom. With only twenty-four hours to solve the case, he must work faster than ever before. Using a tactic of elimination, Hercule pits one family member against the other until the real murderer becomes clear.

> 4 ounces añejo tequila (I recommend Patrón Añejo)
> 1 ounce orange liqueur (I recommend Patrón Citrónge Orange)
> ½ ounce Basic Simple Syrup (page 6)
> 2 ounces orange juice
> ½ ounce lemon juice
> 4 dashes bitters (I recommend Mister Bitters Negroni Bitters)
> Orange slices for garnish

In a bar glass filled with ice, combine all ingredients. Shake well and strain into ice-filled glasses. Garnish with orange slices and serve.

Mocktail

Replace the tequila with Ritual Tequila Alternative or another non-alcoholic spirit, the orange liqueur with Lyre's Italian Orange or another nonalcoholic aperitif, and the bitters with All The Bitter Orange Bitters or other nonalcoholic bitters. Prepare as above.

SANGRIA BONITA

(The Hollow)

Serve 4

Lady Angkatell, long fascinated by the criminal mind, has invited Hercule Poirot to her country estate for a weekend house party with extended family. Things go off with a bang when he arrives to the poolside gathering to find a murder mystery game staged for his amusement. To everyone's horror, the doctor ends up dead in a pool of his own blood, and his wife Gerda is standing over him with a gun, in shock. This is a pool party that has sunk to new lows. As other possible murder weapons surface, so does a tangled web of romantic liaisons, jealousy, and broken hearts. To what lengths will this family go to protect the guilty and cover up the truth? Mix up a batch of family sized Sangria and see you if you can untangle the web of lies!

1 (75-milliliter) bottle sauvignon blanc

4 ounces apricot brandy

4 ounces peach liqueur (I recommend Heimat)

4 ounces Mint Simple Syrup (page 6)

6 strawberries, hulled and sliced

2 star fruits, sliced

1 peach, sliced

Prosecco to top pitcher

In a pitcher filled with ice, combine the sauvignon blanc, brandy, liqueur, and Mint Simple Syrup. Stir to mix. Add in the fruit and stir once more. Top with prosecco and serve.

Mocktail

Replace the sauvignon blanc with Chateau de Fleur or another non-alcoholic sparkling wine, the brandy with apricot nectar, the peach liqueur with peach nectar, and the prosecco with Wölffer Estate Spring in a Bottle or another nonalcoholic prosecco. Prepare as above.

KINGFISHER HILL HOT TODDY

(The Killings at Kingfisher Hill)

◆

Serve 2

Hercule Poirot is traveling with his friend Inspector Edward Catchpool from London to Richard Devonport's grand Kingfisher Hill estate under the pretense of potentially investing in Richard's company. The real reason for their visit, concealed from Richard's family, is to prove that Richard's fiancé, Helen, is innocent of the murder of his brother, Frank. Hercule only has days to investigate before Helen is hanged. Gasp! On the train, a woman demands to get off, insisting that if she stays in her seat, she will be murdered. Hercule and Catchpool take notice, and when murder takes place at Kingfisher Hill, they wonder if the two are tied together. Things are getting hot at Kingfisher Hill.

4 ounces spiced apple cider

½ ounce pineapple juice

¾ ounce Winter Spice Syrup (page 7)

4 ounces rum (I recommend Plantation)

Cinnamon sticks for garnish

In a medium saucepan, combine the cider, pineapple juice, and Winter Spice Syrup and bring to a simmer. Take the saucepan off the heat and add in the rum. Pour into mugs, garnish with cinnamon sticks, and serve.

Mocktail

Replace the rum with Ritual Rum Alternative Zero Proof or another nonalcoholic spirit. Prepare as above.

COOL CAT COCOA

(Third Girl)

◆

Serve 2

In London, three girls share a flat; one is a secretary; the second works in an art gallery, and the third, Norma, approaches Hercule Poirot at a café while he is enjoying his breakfast of brioche and hot chocolate, confesses that she is a murderer, then promptly disappears, thinking that the famous detective is far too old to help her. As Hercule ponders this unconventional encounter, his hot chocolate goes cold. Agatha's recurring character Adriadne Oliver sent Norma to Hercule, and Ariadne pairs up with him to solve this interesting case. In the meantime, Norma's estranged father is back on the scene with his new wife. Gaslighting, drugs, forged art, absentee fathers, horrible roommates, unwanted stepmothers, and untrustworthy boyfriends. Is this a game of offing people to secure an inheritance? Why can't Norma seem to remember certain chunks of time? There's more to this case than miniskirts, so let's get groovy and mix up a batch of warm and toasty cocktails. Can you dig it?

8 ounces hot chocolate

2 teaspoons cinnamon

4 dashes chocolate bitters

4 ounces Drambuie or scotch of choice

Fresh whipped cream to top glasses

2 ounces dark chocolate, grated, for garnish

In a small saucepan, bring the hot chocolate, cinnamon, and bitters to a simmer. Add the Drambuie or scotch of choice and heat through. Pour into mugs or glasses and top with fresh whipped cream. Garnish with dark chocolate and serve.

Mocktail

Replace the Drambuie with Kentucky 74 or another nonalcoholic spirit and the bitters with El Guapo Spiced Cocoa Bitters or other nonalcoholic bitters. Prepare as above.

HICKORY DICKORY DAIQUIRI

(Hickory Dickory Dock)

◆

Serve 2

This title is another nod to Agatha's love of nursery rhymes. Hercule Poirot is asked to investigate a string of petty thefts at a student hostel that include a box of chocolates, a slashed backpack, and a stethoscope. When one student ends up dead, Hercule discovers that another of the students has a bet to acquire three deadly poisons, one now missing. Can Hercule solve the case before the clock strikes twelve?

4 ounces light rum (I recommend Plantation)

2 ounces coconut rum

4 ounces pineapple juice

2 ounces fresh lime juice

1½ cups frozen berries

Dark rum for floater, if desired

Fresh blueberries for garnish

In a blender, combine all ingredients with 1½ cups ice. Blend until smooth and pour into glasses. If desired, add a floater of dark rum to each glass. Skewer fresh blueberries with cocktail picks to garnish, then serve.

Mocktail

Replace the rum(s) with ISH Caribbean Spiced Spirit or another non-alcoholic spirit and the coconut rum with coconut milk or coconut cream. Prepare as above.

MANHATTANS ARE EASY

(Murder Is Easy)

◆

Serve 2

Ex-officer Luke Fitzwilliam strikes up a conversation with little old lady Lavinia Pinkerton on a train to London. Thinking they would chat about the weather, she explains in detail three murders that have taken place, proclaiming the next victim to be Dr. John Humbleby. Fitzwilliam shrugs her off like a little old lady telling tall tales, but the next day reads in the newspaper of her death and the death of Dr. Humbleby. Something is quite off. Can Fitzwilliam solve the case before the next victim falls prey to the killer? Manhattans for the win . . . revenge is tasty.

4 ounces rye whiskey

2 ounces sweet vermouth

4 dashes angostura bitters

Brandied cherries or lemon twists for garnish

In a bar glass filled with ice, combine all ingredients. Stir to chill. Strain into glasses, garnish with cherries or lemon twists, and serve.

Mocktail

Replace the rye whiskey with WhistlePig Rye Non-Whiskey or another nonalcoholic spirit, the vermouth with Lyre's Aperitif Rosso or another nonalcoholic vermouth, and the bitters with All The Bitter Orange Bitters or other nonalcoholic bitters. Prepare as above.

THE MOUSETRAP

A gatha's *The Mousetrap* is the longest-running show of any kind in the world. It opened in November 1952 at the Ambassadors Theatre in London and moved to St. Martin's Theatre in March 1974 where it is still running to this day. It has been performed in twenty-seven languages in more than fifty countries. A favorite of the royals, Her Majesty Queen Elizabeth II attended the fiftieth anniversary performance on November 25, 2002. The play is set to make its Broadway debut in 2023.

BLACK VELVET CURTAINS

(The Mousetrap)

— ◆ —

Serve 2

The scene is set when a group of people gathered in a country house are cut off by the snow and discover, to their horror, that there is a murderer in their midst. Who can it be? One by one the suspicious characters reveal their sordid pasts until the last, nerve-shredding moment when the killer's identity and motive are finally revealed. The play is known for keeping the murderer under wraps by asking the audience after each performance to keep the secret for future theatergoers. This cocktail is a classic mix of rich flavor and decadence, reflecting all there is to love about the entertainment, intrigue, and mystery of the world's longest-running play.

> 1 pint chilled Guinness
> Chilled brut champagne to top glasses

In two flute glasses, pour the Guinness halfway. Float the brut champagne layer (see on page 11) by pouring the brut champagne over the back of a barspoon into each flute glass. Serve.

Mocktail

Replace the Guinness with Guinness 0.0 Non-Alcoholic Stout or another nonalcoholic stout and the brut champagne with Chateau De Fleur or another nonalcoholic brut champagne. Prepare as above.

THE MOUSETRAP

(The Mousetrap)

◆

Serve 2

The Mousetrap *began as a short radio play called* Three Blind Mice *and was written at the request of the BBC for Queen Mary. Agatha worked to expand* Three Blind Mice *from a twenty-minute radio show into a full-length stage play, adding extra characters and a fuller background and plot twists. Finally, the name was changed, and* The Mousetrap *was created. This cocktail has distinct flavors of smoky, sweet, tart, and bitter—much like the characters in Agatha's play. Cheers to another opening night!*

- 4 ounces vodka
- 2 ounces aperol
- 2 ounces elderflower liqueur (I recommend Heimat)
- 1 ounce fresh lime juice
- Sparkling rosé to top glasses
- Edible gold glitter for garnish

In a small pitcher, combine the vodka, aperol, elderflower liqueur, and lime juice. Refrigerate for up to thirty minutes. Add mixture to flute glasses and top with sparkling rosé. Garnish with edible gold glitter and serve.

Mocktail

Replace the sparkling rosé with Wölffer Estate Spring in a Bottle or another nonalcoholic wine, the vodka with Monday or another nonalcoholic spirit, the aperol with Wilfred's Bitter Orange or another nonalcoholic aperol, and the elderflower liqueur with De Soi or another nonalcoholic aperitif. Prepare as above.

DETECTIVE DRINKING GAMES & TRIVIA

Perfect Match

Each quote below comes from one of Agatha's novels or from Agatha herself. Each player takes a turn reading a quote aloud, then choosing another player to name the character and novel. If the player guesses the right character but wrong novel, they drink; wrong character but right novel, they drink; neither correct, everyone drinks! Answers are on page 116.

1. "Imagination is a good servant, and a bad master. The simplest explanation is always the most likely."
2. "Ah, but my dear sir, the why must never be obvious. That is the whole point."
3. "When the Sun shines you cannot see the moon," he said. "But when the sun is gone—ah, when the sun is gone."
4. "We cannot catch a train earlier than the time that it leaves, and to ruin one's clothes will not be the least bit helpful in preventing a murder."
5. "I know there's a proverb which says, 'To err is human' but a human error is nothing to what a computer can do if it tries."
6. "Gentlemen . . . are frequently not as level-headed as they seem."
7. "It really is very dangerous to believe people. I never have for years."
8. "I know that in books it is always the most unlikely person. But I never find that rule applies in real life."

(continued . . .)

9. "If people do not choose to lower their voices, one must assume that they are prepared to be overheard."
10. "To every problem, there is a most simple solution."
11. "Good advice is always certain to be ignored, but that's no reason not to give it."
12. "Crime is terribly revealing. Try and vary your methods as you will, your tastes, your habits, your attitude of mind, and your soul is revealed by your actions."
13. "Every murderer is probably somebody's old friend."

True or False

Wrong answers, drink.

1. Poison was the cause of death for more than thirty of Agatha's characters.
2. Agatha Christie was a shy and private person.
3. Agatha's play, *The Mousetrap*, closed after two weeks.
4. Agatha was a fan of wigs.
5. Agatha's house, Greenway in Devon, was occupied by the US Naval Intelligence during WWII as an officer's mess. It was there that plans for the D-Day invasion were solidified.
6. Agatha studied literature while attending university.
7. Hercule Poirot, when his character died, had a full-page obituary in *The New York Times*.
8. Agatha's nephew got the rights to *The Mousetrap* when he was nine.
9. Agatha disappeared for eleven days in 1935.

How Well Do You Know Agatha?

If you get the answer wrong, you drink. If no one in the group gets the answer, everyone drinks.

1. Favorite color
2. Favorite cocktail
3. Favorite house
4. Favorite book she wrote
5. Least favorite character she wrote
6. Agatha's bestselling book
7. Birth year
8. Favorite place to travel
9. Fastest crime novel she wrote
10. Favorite hobby
11. Favorite food
12. Favorite flower

ANSWERS

Perfect Match

1. Character: Hercule Poirot
   Novel: *The Mysterious Affair at Styles*
2. Character: Hercule Poirot
   Novel: *Five Little Pigs*
3. Character: Hercule Poirot
   Novel: *Death on the Nile*
4. Character: Hercule Poirot
   Novel: *The ABC Murders*
5. Character: Hercule Poirot
   Novel: *Hallowe'en Party*
6. Character: Miss Marple
   Novel: *The Body in the Library*
7. Character: Miss Marple
   Novel: *Sleeping Murder*
8. Character: Miss Marple
   Novel: *The Murder at the Vicarage*
9. Character: Miss Marple
   Novel: *At Bertram's Hotel*
10. Agatha Christie
11. Agatha Christie
12. Agatha Christie
13. Agatha Christie

True or False

1. True
2. True

3. False: *The Mousetrap* is the world's longest-running play
4. True
5. True
6. False: Agatha never attended school; she taught herself how to read and write
7. True
8. True
9. False: 1926

How Well Do You Know Agatha?

1. Green.
2. Agatha didn't drink.
3. Greenway in Devon.
4. It varied as she reread them. Her last list included *And Then There Were None* and *The Murder of Roger Ackroyd*.
5. Hercule Poirot. Agatha considered him "detestable, bombastic, and tiresome" but he was the most storied and memorable character of her illustrious writing career so she knew better to keep him in her books.
6. *And Then There Were None*, with more than 100 million copies sold.
7. 1890.
8. Egypt, although she was a world traveler. There are several travel companies that offer Agatha Christie travel tours.
9. It took Agatha just two weeks to write *The Mysterious Affair at Styles* and only three days to write *Absent in the Spring*, the third of six novels under the pen name Mary Westmacott.
10. Gardening.
11. Clotted Cream (although more of a drink than food).
12. Lily of the valley.

ACKNOWLEDGMENTS

Special thanks to all who helped put this book together. It was amazing to work with each and every one of you.

Thank you to my editor Nicole Mele, who is an avid Christie fan and was game from the word go, and to my talented cover designer Kai Texel.

Thanks to my agent Marilyn Allen, who saw potential in bringing this idea to market and was confident it would find the right home.

Special thanks to my brilliant friend and photographer Jack Deutsch, with whom I've worked on various projects for over twenty years, whose talents and tireless energy brought these cocktails to life. Thanks to stylist Jessica Saal for graciously lending your talents and time to the shoot.

To Kemper Donovan, I learn so much from your podcasts. Thank you for sharing your knowledge and for writing a fabulous foreword.

And to my family who once again lived through recipe testing and tasting, the influx of glassware, barware, props, and bottles of simple syrups taking over the refrigerator, thank you for your support. It's funny how we've migrated from tutus and truck parties to watermelon margaritas and cocktail gardens. What a team we make.

Colleen Mullaney is a well-known lifestyle expert and bestselling author of books covering a range of topics on entertaining, cocktails, floral design, and weddings. Her most recent, *Gin Austen,* won the International Gourmand Drink Culture Award. Her other sought-after cocktail books include *It's Five o'Clock Somewhere, Punch,* and *The Stylish Girl's Guide to Fabulous Cocktails.*

A former magazine editor-in-chief, Colleen has gone on to create interiors for residential, commercial, and hospitality spaces, and has designed floral arrangements and cottage gardens for her many clients. She is a regular contributor to *Huffington Post* and Today.com and has been featured on HGTV's *Insider's Garden,* Martha Stewart Radio, and in *InStyle, New York Daily News,* and *Woman's Day,* among others.

Colleen lives in Westchester, New York, with her husband and three children.

METRIC CONVERSIONS

Term	Measurement (Imperial)	Measurement (Metric)
1 part	Any equal part	Any equal part
1 dash	⅟₃₂ ounce	1 milliliter
1 teaspoon	⅕ ounce	6 milliliters
1 tablespoon	⅙ ounce	5 milliliters
1 pony	½ ounce	15 milliliters
1 jigger/shot	1 ounce	30 milliliters
1 snit	3 ounces	90 milliliters
1 wine glass	4 ounces	120 milliliters
1 split	6 ounces	180 milliliters
1 cup	8 ounces	240 milliliters
1 pint	16 ounces	475 milliliters

INDEX